BLESSED ARE YOU

Blessed Are You
Mother Teresa and the Beatitudes

Prepared and Edited by
Eileen Egan
and
Kathleen Egan, O.S.B.

Servant Publications
Ann Arbor, Michigan

Never let anything
so fill you
with pain or sorrow
so as to make you forget
the joy
of Christ Risen.

Mother Teresa

Published by Servant Publications
P.O. Box 8617
Ann Arbor, Michigan 48107

Scripture texts used in this work, unless otherwise indicated, are taken from the *Revised Standard Version* of the Bible, copyright © 1946, 1952, and 1971, by the Division of Christian Education of the National Council of Churches of Christ in the U.S.A., and are used by permission.

Cover design by Michael Andaloro
Cover photo by Lawrence Jankowski
Text design by K. Kelly Nelson

92 93 94 95 96 10 9 8 7 6 5 4 3 2

Printed in the United States of America
ISBN 0-89283-743-8

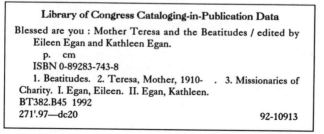

Library of Congress Cataloging-in-Publication Data

Blessed are you : Mother Teresa and the Beatitudes / edited by
    Eileen Egan and Kathleen Egan.
        p.   cm
    ISBN 0-89283-743-8
    1. Beatitudes. 2. Teresa, Mother, 1910-   . 3. Missionaries of
Charity. I. Egan, Eileen. II. Egan, Kathleen.
BT382.B45 1992
271'.97—dc20
                                                        92-10913

Contents

Introduction

THE BEATITUDES are inseparable from the Sermon on the Mount, which has been called the very core of the Christian message. Through them Jesus taught his hearers about Gospel values, which are just as applicable today as they were then. Meditating and reflecting on the Beatitudes will help us apply those values to our daily lives. But to help the Beatitudes come alive for us we need models.

Mother Teresa, a humble follower of Jesus, serves as an inspiring witness in daily living the Beatitudes. Her example may help to resolve the paradox of the Beatitudes. Her life, her words, and her experiences help us to have a vision of the hope and joy implicit in the promises of the Beatitudes, even when we are called to suffer. She spends her life expressing the love brought by Jesus, a love that necessarily involves the cross.

In each chapter, *Words to Ponder* offers a short meditation on one of the Beatitudes and its promise. These insights seek to elicit reflection and meditation from the reader in facing the seeming dilemma of the Beatitudes with faith, hope, and love.

In the next section, *Mother Teresa in Her Own Words*, this woman of faith shares her own reflections on the Beatitude. In the final section, *Living the Beatitudes*, we glimpse how Mother Teresa and her order, the Missionaries of Charity, bring this love into the farthest corners of our world.

Mother Teresa puts flesh on all the Beatitudes. While she is truly a woman of the Beatitudes, she personifies in a special way "Blessed are the merciful." In her, the world sees the very incarnation of mercy, a quality hungered for in an age of the mercilessness of wars and the build-up of weapons of mass destruction that threaten the human family. The same mercy that overcomes all the barriers of race, creed, or nation is possible to each of us. We can be moved to make it a part of our lives by remembering those who cry out for our help.

THE SHOCK OF THE BEATITUDES

Why do we moderns, even if we are Christians, find the Beatitudes so shocking? Perhaps it will help us to return in spirit to the site where Jesus is thought to have preached his famous sermon on the Mount. There the Chapel of the Beatitudes stands on a mount near the Sea of Galilee, still a peaceful pastoral setting. For many, it is one of the most beautiful spots on the face of the globe. The chapel reminds us of that day when Jesus sat among his disciples and a crowd gathered to hear him speak. "Opening his mouth, he taught them" (Mt 5:2), Matthew tells us.

It is consoling to realize that Jesus' sermon shocked his own hearers. In the Beatitudes Jesus turned upside down some of the values by which people of every age live, even those of us in the modern world today.

The disciples of Jesus were accustomed to the form of the Beatitudes. It is a form of expression that abounds in the Hebrew Scriptures.

"Happy [are] those who keep my ways" is found in Proverbs 8:33. "Blessed" carries the same meaning as "happy" or "fortunate." It is a declaration of happiness on the grounds of righteousness or good fortune.

However, in the Beatitudes, which introduce the Sermon on the Mount, Jesus astounds his hearers. He applies the declaration of happiness to situations far beyond what the world considers good, namely mercy and peacemaking. He speaks of what the world considers evil—poverty, hunger, sorrow, and even persecution.

These words are followed by the shocking words of Jesus in Matthew 5:12 and Luke 6:23: "Rejoice and exult."

Rejoice in sorrow and in persecution? Jesus was preparing his followers for a dramatically new way to respond to daily life. Jesus called himself "The Way," leading to Truth and Life. Eventually his followers were called "People of the Way."

How can the "People of the Way" rejoice in sorrow and even in persecution? A key, as we shall see, is the promise accompanying each of the Beatitudes.

A HUMBLE BEGINNING AND A SHOCKING CALL

When a small woman stepped out on the streets of a scourged city wearing the rough cotton sari of the poor, her bare feet in sandals, she shocked those around her. She had followed the call to religious life, becoming a model nun and an admired teacher in a teaching congregation.

Suddenly she was alone on the street, having sensed a call to serve the poorest of the poor, her traditional habit a thing of the past. An inspiration had moved Mother Teresa to leave the enclosed life, with permission of her superiors, "to listen to the cry of the poor" on the open street.

In this new call, in the late 1940s, Sister Teresa (later to become Mother Teresa) lived through the days of the Great Killing in Calcutta, during the partition of India. Thousands perished on the blood-spattered streets. Smoke from the funeral pyres filled the air. But the agony of a million refugees lived on after the violence subsided.

What could a woman, alone and without resources, do in such a setting?

Not only was her appearance startling, but her utter dependence on the power of God was shocking to less venturesome souls. Mother Teresa detached herself from the loving community of the Loreto Sisters, the teaching order to which she belonged, even though it was so dear to her. She detached herself from the security of the planned, though demanding and austere, life of a teaching Sister.

Mother Teresa directed her steps to one of the worst slums of the refugee-choked city. She gathered the near-naked children around her and taught them to read. She drilled them, by rote, in the Bengali alphabet, forming the letters with a stick in the dusty earth.

Two of her former students joined her, following her example of wearing the cheapest of cotton saris. They opened a school in rented, dirt-floored rooms. A Bengali Catholic family gave them shelter.

As they made their way to their primitive school, they saw men, women, and children, famished and near death, lying on the sidewalks.

Mother Teresa's simple response was, *"We cannot let the children of God die like animals in the gutter."* They brought the dying to rented rooms where, served by tender hands, they could at least die with dignity.

From such a simple and humble beginning arose a new religious family, the Missionaries of Charity. Their aim was to bring the love of Jesus to the "poorest of the poor" in the human family—to the destitute dying, the famished, the homeless, the lepers, the victims of AIDS, and those unwanted, even in today's affluent societies.

Application for Today. How does this apply to Christians living in the modern world today, especially lay people who are not under vows? Everyone at one time or another has received an inspiration, perhaps no more than an impulse, to serve the suffering and the needy. This impulse should not be ignored but acted upon, even if it calls for the smallest act of mercy.

Being "poor in spirit" may involve detaching ourselves from the satisfaction of personal needs, or from possessions and associations that provide pleasure or acceptance. Responding to the impulse or inspiration may then rest on dependence on God and his providence.

We will become ready to use our own poor means, whatever may be at our disposal. As Mother Teresa told me, *"If I had not picked up that first person dying on the street, I would not have picked up the thousands later on."*

The question of success should be irrelevant. *"We are not called to be successful,"* Mother Teresa keeps repeating, *"we are called to be faithful."*

A WOMAN OF THE BEATITUDES TODAY

Meeting Mother Teresa. A few years after Mother Teresa opened the "Home for the Dying" (in a pilgrim's hostel at the temple of the goddess Kali), I[1] walked from pallet to pallet with her. Daily, forsaken human beings were brought to the

---

1. The use of the first-person singular pronoun throughout the text refers to Eileen Egan who traveled and served with Mother Teresa for over thirty years.

home to have the filth and spittle of the gutter washed away, to have their sores cleaned and dressed. I saw with what infinite patience the Missionaries of Charity nursed the spark of life in near-corpses.

"How can you do this day after day?" I asked Mother Teresa.

"They are Jesus," she replied. *"Each one is Jesus in a distressing disguise."*

She viewed each one, I realized, in the light of the Incarnation, that light brought by Jesus, when he took on our flesh and blood and bone. In that light, Mother Teresa saw beyond the body disfigured by disease and hideous sores, to the divinity within. She saw in each, infinite, inviolable worth, the worth of a person for whom a Person died. The Person, Jesus, who had willingly died out of love for humankind, had told his followers, "Such as my love has been for you, so must your love be for each other" (Jn 13:34). His love included the cross. In place after place, this has been Mother Teresa's witness, even in our changing world of today.

Mother Teresa in Europe. The great upheaval in Eastern Europe came in 1989 when oppressive regimes of communism fell, one by one, nonviolently. People freed themselves by acts of community cooperation, led by people of conscience who had endured jail terms for their beliefs.

As one of the Calcutta Sisters wrote, "Nothing could hold Mother Teresa. She was off to Eastern Europe." The Sisters were already at work in Poland, the former East Germany, Hungary, and Yugoslavia.

Speaking from Rome, Mother Teresa told me: *"I have just come back from Romania and Czechoslovakia. Romania is so poor, so terribly poor."* Her voice reflected her concern for such suffering as she had seen nowhere else in Europe.

"Our Sisters are already in Bucharest. They will work with those poor children in the institutions." The tragic eyes of little Romanian children had been seen staring into the television cameras.

As history opens doors for the expression of the love brought by Jesus in merciful service, Mother Teresa and the Sisters hurry through.

I mentioned to Mother Teresa that the Albanian government announced at the United Nations a change in its laws to allow freedom to believers. I said there was hope that she would soon take her Sisters there.

"It will come. It will come," said Mother Teresa. "It will come in God's time."

"God's time" came soon, when the Albanian government

announced that the atheist constitution would be formally changed. This would allow the opening of long-closed churches and mosques.

The film, "Mother Teresa," made by Ann and Jeanette Petrie, was shown to a large audience in Tirana, Albania, an audience which included persons in government ministries. Mother Teresa was able to kneel at the grave of her mother and sister, when she brought her first team of Missionaries of Charity to Tirana in 1991.

Four teams followed to bring help to the people of Europe's poorest and most forlorn country. One building offered to Mother Teresa for her work was a mosque. She refused it, saying it should be given back to the Muslims.

Mother Teresa in the Former Soviet Union. When in the former Soviet Union all human need and all welfare was placed in state control, relief of suffering was torn from the hands of Christian believers. As the Soviet system revealed its tragic failures, Mother Teresa was among the first invited into a great empire in collapse, to perform the simple works of mercy that Jesus taught his followers.

The Sisters chose the most helpless among Moscow's people to start their work, a hospital for multi-handicapped children.

The founding of the Moscow house took place in 1988, a momentous year celebrating one thousand years since the introduction of Christianity in Russia (referred to as the Millennium). It was just after the seventieth anniversary of the revolution, during which Christianity entered a dark period. Thousands of churches and monasteries had been closed, destroyed, or turned into warehouses or museums.

As freedom has been restored to the churches in Russia, a group of Orthodox believers formed a society called simply *Miloserdiye,* or "Mercy." With almost no resources, they organized themselves to find ways to meet the needs of those most deprived.

After Moscow, teams of the Missionaries of Charity carried the work to Leningrad, in the Gulf of Finland, to earthquake-ravaged Armenia, to Tbilisi, in Georgia (where Stalin attended a seminary), and even to Novosibirsk, Siberia. Mother Teresa had achieved an invasion of *Miloserdiye* in the great expanse of the former Soviet Union, where Christian mercy had long been outlawed. It was nothing less than a revolution of mercy, in which the former Soviet citizens, now freed from the shackles of an anti-religious regime, were engaged.

"Mother, you are sending your Sisters to Siberia," I remarked to her, in May 1990.

"Yes," said Mother Teresa happily. *"This one in Novosibirsk is our sixth house in the Soviet Union. We have been asked to open seven more."*

To many, the dread word, Siberia, connotes a place of punishment, exile, and death.

It must have been a strange sight when a team of Indian Missionaries of Charity, each in her white sari and sandals, arrived in Novosibirsk to "listen to the cry of the poor." As usual when they enter cold climates, the Sisters wore heavy socks under their sandals, and layers of garments against the receding snows of April.

A Lithuanian Franciscan priest had prepared for their coming. He took them to a spare apartment in a housing complex. They would begin their work with orphans and needy children. He had received permission to build a center for children in a birch forest outside Novosibirsk.

Such is the witness of Mother Teresa and her Missionaries of Charity in the far corners of the world, even in the former bastions of atheism and communism. Such was the witness of Jesus in his day, from the dusty roads of Galilee to the inner precincts of the temple in Jerusalem. Such should be our way, whoever we are and wherever we are called to serve.

The Beatitudes

Seeing the crowds,
he went up
on the mountain,
and when he sat down,
his disciples
came to him.

Mother Teresa kneels after receiving Communion.

Blessed
are
the poor
in spirit,
for theirs is
the kingdom
of heaven.

ONE

Blessed Are
the Poor in Spirit

WORDS TO PONDER

Seeing the crowds, he went up on the mountain, and when he sat down his disciples came to him. And he opened his mouth and he taught them, saying: "Blessed are the poor in spirit, for theirs is the kingdom of heaven." Mt 5:1-3

All the other Beatitudes depend on this first one. It is only by being transformed in spirit, by recognizing both our total inadequacy and the almighty power of God, that we can find the door to his kingdom.

St. Paul describes the utmost in poverty of spirit:

Have this mind among yourselves, which is yours in Christ Jesus, who, though he was in the form of God, did not count equality with God a thing to be grasped, but emptied himself, taking the form of a servant, being born in the likeness of men. Phil 2:5-7

This emptying is echoed in the Rule written for her Sisters by Mother Teresa. Describing Christ's call to poverty, she wrote:

Christ, who being rich became poor and emptied Himself to work out our redemption, calls us:

to share in his poverty so that we might become rich through His poverty;

to bear witness to the true face of Jesus—poor, humble, and friend of sinners, the weak and the despised—and to the Church of the poor whose mission is to preach the Gospel to the poor;

to listen to the cry of the poor, especially in our times, which urges us to make reparation for the selfishness and greed of man, craving for

earthly riches and power to the point of
injustice to others. —From the Rule of the Missionaries of Charity

Lord Jesus,
We know that you became poor for our sake.
We ask that you make us to be poor in spirit,
to imitate your own confident dependence
on your Father. Your promise
is the very kingdom of your Father,
whom you taught us to call "Our Father."
We ask you to lead us in caring for those other poor
ones in our life.
We know that on our action
depends our Father's judgment
at our death.

MOTHER TERESA IN HER OWN WORDS

The Rule of the Missionaries of Charity serves as the official rule guiding the formation and life of the Sisters. It comes from the spirit and vision of Mother Teresa. Every Missionary of Charity has a copy of the rule. Mother Teresa said: *"I must cling to the rule as a child clings to its mother. I must love the rule with my soul and body."*

This message of Mother Teresa carries illumination not only for the Sisters and for persons under vows, but for all who would be poor in spirit.

Our response to the call of Christ is our vow of poverty. This entails a life which is poor in reality and in spirit, sober and industrious, and a stranger to earthly riches. It also involves dependence and limitation in the use and disposition of goods.

By this vow we freely give to God our natural right and freedom to accept and to dispose freely of anything that has a monetary value. Therefore, we shall never keep, give away, lend or borrow things of money value without leave of the Superior.

With regard to God, our poverty is our humble recognition and acceptance of our sinfulness, helplessness and utter nothingness, and the acknowledgement of our neediness before Him, which expresses itself as hope in Him, as an openness to receive all things from Him as from our Father.

Our poverty should be true Gospel poverty: gentle, tender, glad and openhearted, always ready to give an expression of love. Poverty is love before it is renunciation: To love it is necessary to give. To give, it is necessary to be free from selfishness.

We rejoice with Our Blessed Lady who sang so truthfully: "He has filled the hungry with good things, the rich he has sent empty away." —From the Rule of the Missionaries of Charity

LIVING THE BEATITUDES

Turning off Calcutta's Lower Circular Road, roaring with trolley cars and the cries of hawkers, I found the doorway of the Missionaries of Charity Convent on a side alley. I pulled a rope. In answer to the clang of a large bell, a young woman clad in a sari appeared. A few minutes later, Mother Teresa greeted me. A short vigorous woman with a luminous smile, she led me into a spare parlor. We sat at a rickety table. I told her I came from Catholic Relief Services, the overseas arm of the American Catholic community.

It was in October 1955, five years after she had founded the Missionaries of Charity. After that day my life was never the same. "*I will show you our people*," Mother Teresa said. During my first limited visit to Calcutta, I saw, with mounting horror, life in the open streets, life in a cluster of lepers' homes in one of the thousands of slums or "bustees" that ringed the city, and death in the Home for the Dying.

As I shuddered at the rows of near-skeletons in the men's and women's wards, Mother Teresa leaned over to console them in Hindi and in Bengali. Some even managed to return her smile as she took their skeletonized hands in hers. *"These are our treasures,"* she said. *"Each is Jesus in a distressing disguise."*

Charged with the program for India at the headquarters of Catholic Relief Services, I saw how the generosity of American Catholics made a difference in the lives of the poorest of the poor in Calcutta.

A city of need from the beginning, Calcutta became "the slum of the world" when a million destitute refugees arrived in 1947. They poured in from across the partition border with Pakistan, continuing to bring their burden of need to the city every day of the year.

It was not until 1965 that Mother Teresa was permitted to take teams of the Missionaries of Charity outside of India. In response to a bishop's invitation, Mother Teresa decided to bring a team of Sisters to a needy area of Venezuela. Mother Teresa asked Bishop Edward Swanstrom of Catholic Relief Services, if I could act as her companion since I spoke Spanish. I could also carry out a program for CRS.

The first team started their work among the old, the ill, and the needy of Cocorote on July 25, 1965. Mother Teresa and I had traveled from village to village and town to town before she settled on that town. Later, Cocorote would become a center from which Sisters went out to establish seven houses in every part of Venezuela.

To mark the twenty-fifth anniversary of the arrival of the Missionaries of Charity in Venezuela, I wrote to Mother Teresa telling her of my joy at the founding of many houses since that date. In twenty-five years, she crisscrossed the world, responding to invitations to bring Sisters to every continent. At the same time, the Sisters intensified their work for the neediest in many of India's cities.

I received a reply from Mother Teresa which put into a few words the very core of her belief and message. Experiencing the utmost in poverty of spirit, she detached herself completely from the achievement. She rejoiced that since Cocorote, the Sisters had opened four hundred houses, one hundred sixty-four in India and two hundred seventy-six houses overseas in ninety-four countries. Then she made a simple, characteristic comment, *"What wonders God has done with nothingness."*

A stupendous achievement, if viewed in human terms, was seen, with the eye of the spirit, as something else—as the work of a loving Creator. At the same time, Mother Teresa sees herself as the instrument of the Creator, repeating: "*I am only a pencil in God's hand.... God writes through us, and however imperfect instruments we may be, God writes beautifully.*"

The Simplicity of the Messenger. Mother Teresa has been likened to one particular saint more than to any other in the history of Christianity: St. Francis, the poor man of Assisi. In June 1982 during the year marking eight hundred years since the birth of St. Francis, Mother Teresa was invited to San Francisco, the city named for this saint. An evening benediction was held at the Cathedral of St. Mary. So packed was the Cathedral that security guards were everywhere trying to keep order.

Author Dale Vree was present and wrote this account:

"How odd that this founder of the Missionaries of Charity —an order given not to preaching but to doing the Word— should be preaching! Women don't have an important role in the Church, it is said, and here is (literally) a little old lady, not quite in tennis shoes but in sandals, preaching to ecclesi-astics and magistrates. Why am I almost in tears?"

He said, "Maybe because she's one of those who indu-bitably earned a right to proclaim the gospel. And more, the gospel simplicity of the message is matched by the gospel simplicity of the messenger."

Later when one of the journalists asked what it feels like to be called a "living saint," she responded: *"I'm very happy if you can see Jesus in me, because I can see Jesus in you. Holiness is not just for a few people. It's for everyone, including you, sir."*

Only a Thank You to God. *"Simplicity. No expenses, no con-certs, no decorations, only a thank you to God,"* was the way Mother Teresa wanted the thanksgiving celebrations of the Order's Twenty-fifth Jubilee. *"I ask each religious group to hold its own thanksgiving service, to acknowledge that God is our central figure, that this is His work and not ours."*

Members of eighteen different religions united in a single act of thanksgiving in one week. Beautiful, prayerful cere-monies occurred in the various Christian churches and other places of worship in Calcutta. To each of them Mother Teresa and her Sisters were invited.

During the week-long jubilee, a hidden event deeply impressed Mother Teresa. As an act of penance (for the intentions of Mother Teresa), a Jain nun chose to pull out hair from her head. When Mother Teresa arrived at the Jain temple, she was so moved with compassion by this offering that she too pulled out a couple of hairs from her own head and accepted the pain—as a sign of love and solidarity. We are reminded of the widow in the temple putting her mite—all that she had—in the offering box. That's Gospel poverty.

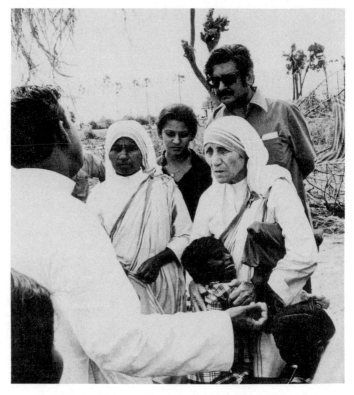

Mother Teresa aids cyclone victims in India.

Blessed
are those
who mourn,
for they
shall be
comforted.

Blessed Are
Those Who Mourn

WORDS TO PONDER

Blessed are those who mourn, for they shall be comforted.

Mt 5:4

All the Beatitudes are something to live by, and something
to live for. This beautiful Beatitude, also rendered as "Blessed
are the sorrowing," is perhaps the most difficult and most mysterious.

"I am the Way," Jesus taught his followers; it is clear that
the pathway would not be a smooth one. The abiding com-

fort of the Christian is that Jesus, the Messiah, the Incarnate God, has walked the path before us.

Mother Teresa gives us an example of a way to find comfort in a time of mourning and sorrow: give comfort to others.

How can we feel blessed (with its undertone of being happy) when we are tempted almost beyond our strength? When people make fun of us? When a friend rejects or even betrays us? When we are beset by loneliness or plagued by failure?

Lord Jesus,
We have known grief and bereavement,
and we have experienced your consolation.
We want to share that consolation with
those who are now mourning.
Help us to find ways to show compassion
to the sorrowful, the lonely, the deprived,
to those in darkness, in despair.
Help us to recall your dying for us,
knowing that the overwhelming comfort
is your Resurrection.

Death came close to Mother Teresa in Rome in June 1983. She was rushed to a hospital where a doctor made a preliminary examination. She had come near to a heart attack. At first she was not allowed to raise her arms, and had to be fed by others. When her strength began to return, she wrote out the fruit of her meditation. Always Jesus was to be served in the poorest members of God's human family.

For those who lie prone in illness, Mother Teresa's litany can be a prayer of hope. A portion of her litany follows:

Who Is Jesus to Me?

Jesus is the Word made Flesh.
Jesus is the Bread of Life.
Jesus is the Victim offered for our sins on the Cross.
Jesus is the Sacrifice offered at the Holy Mass for
    the sins of the world and mine.
Jesus is the Word—to be spoken.
Jesus is the Truth—to be told.
Jesus is the Way—to be walked.
Jesus is the Light—to be lit.
Jesus is the Life—to be lived.

Jesus is the Love—to be loved.
Jesus is the Joy—to be shared.
Jesus is the Sacrifice—to be offered.
Jesus is the Peace—to be given.
Jesus is the Bread of Life—to be eaten.
Jesus is the Hungry—to be fed.
Jesus is the Thirsty—to be satiated.
Jesus is the Naked—to be clothed.
Jesus is the Homeless—to be taken in.
Jesus is the Sick—to be healed.
Jesus is the Lonely—to be loved.

To Suffering Co-Workers.[1] *Suffering is nothing by itself, but suffering that is shared with the passion of Christ is a wonderful gift and a sign of love. God is very good to give you so much suffering and so much love. All this becomes for me a real joy, and it gives me great strength because of you.*

It is your life of sacrifice that gives me so much strength. Your prayers and suffering are like the chalice in which those of us who work can pour the love of the souls we encounter. So you are just as necessary as we are. We and you together can do all things in him who strengthens.

---

1. See Appendix Two for an explanation of the work of the Co-Workers of Mother Teresa.

How beautiful is your vocation of suffering Co-Workers: you are messengers of God's love. We carry in our hearts the love of God, who is thirsty for souls; you can quench his thirst through your incomparable suffering, to which our hard work is united. It is you who have tasted the chalice of his agony.

The Gift of Smiling. *Without our suffering, our task would be merely a social task, very beautiful and useful, but not Jesus' work. It would not be a part of redemption.*

Jesus has wished to offer us his help by sharing our life, our loneliness, our agony, our death. It was necessary for him to become one with us in order to save us.

We are allowed to do likewise. The afflictions of the poor, not only their material misery but also their spiritual lowliness are to be redeemed. We have to share these afflictions, since only by becoming poor will we be able to save them—that is, to bring God into their lives and to bring them to God.

When suffering comes close to us, let us accept it with a smile. This is God's greatest gift: having the courage to accept with a smile all he gives us and all he requires of us.

Sharing with Christ. *Sacrifice, in order to be genuine, has to empty us of ourselves.*

45

We often say to Christ, Make us partakers of your suffering. But, when someone is insensitive to us, how easily we forget that this is the moment to share with Christ! It would be enough for us to remember that it is Jesus who gives us, through such a person or circumstance, the opportunity to do something beautiful for him.

—From a Co-Worker Meeting, Lippstadt, Germany, 1976

LIVING THE BEATITUDES

On September 8, 1986, the Missionaries of Charity opened the Gift of Peace (a home for AIDS patients) in Washington, D.C. It is one of seven AIDS hopices conducted by the Sisters in the United States. In these homes, the Sisters give care and consolation to those afflicted with the eventually fatal disease. A Sister shared with me the story of Tina, a young victim of AIDS. Tina's story is paraphrased here.

Tina was the first child we had in our Gift of Peace home. She came to us on the Feast of the Holy Innocents, December 28, shortly before her ninth birthday. Both of her parents were drug addicts. She was very proud of her mother who used to visit her on Sunday afternoons, and she would tell our Sisters, "My Mom is here today."

Tina's whole body became a mass of sores, but she often lay on her bed singing:

Jesus loves me, this I know
For the Bible tells me so.
Little ones to him belong.
They are weak but he is strong.
Yes, Jesus loves me.

As Tina's disease became worse, one could barely touch her, because contact caused her so much pain. She was an affectionate child who would say, "Sister, can I give you a kiss?"

We meditated on Tina as a victim; Tina, condemned from the dawn of her reason to a death from AIDS; Tina's hands, made for playing, and bound by the sins of an adult world she did not know; Tina, crucified in her little bed, thirsting in her last hours for a cup of cold water; Tina, giving up her spirit at the age of nine.

God gave us the grace of knowing Tina and mourning with her. Because Jesus loves us so much, he wanted us to see Tina, not as some unfortunate child, but to see the glory of God revealed in her. We could see her as Jesus, the Holy

Innocent, Jesus, the Sacrificial Lamb, Jesus lifted up in glory.

Mary, who saw the precious blood of Jesus spill on the ground, saw the glory of Jesus in the precious moment when others saw only sadness and despair. She can lead us to keep faith at that moment when we are tempted to run from the foot of the cross, from the poor and suffering in front of us.

I Can Be a Counselor. Often people with much to mourn share their stories with Mother Teresa, wishing to get from her a measure of hope. In the home of Co-Worker Leaders, Patty and Warren Kump (in Minnesota), a distressed family brought to her their teenage son. In an accident with fireworks, he had been blinded and had lost both of his hands. The boy explained that the powerful fireworks he and his friends had prepared to use exploded prematurely. He had then fallen from a tree into the flames. His seared eyes were blinded, and his burned hands had had to be amputated.

Mother Teresa sat down on a couch with the boy. As they conversed, she reminded him that his experience helped him to have sympathy for the many thousands who had also lost their sight and the use of their hands. He would understand them, and could help them in a special way.

The boy agreed, "I've been thinking of becoming a counselor," he said, "because I feel I can understand people's sufferings." Mother Teresa said to the now-smiling boy, *"You will make a fine counselor."* Her long experience with difficulties, with tragedies, lent power to her words of encouragement for the boy.

"Yes, I can be a good counselor," he repeated, and his voice carried a note of joy.

Death as Going Home. Because she is a good listener, Mother Teresa seems to give those who come to her the courage they need in their difficulties. Once an older woman was giving her a very large gift of a precious gem which her late husband had bequeathed her.

All of a sudden she interrupted Mother Teresa to say, "I am full of fear. I am afraid of death. You can help me, for you have seen many people die. This is why I wanted to talk to you. You face dying people every day."

Mother Teresa spent time with the fearful lady. They discovered both of their fathers were named Nikola. Mother Teresa expressed thanks for the gift, saying that some Jain friends of hers (gem dealers) would turn the gift into cash. Then she would assign that money for a home for the destitute and dying in Bombay, a home called "Asha Dan."

Mother Teresa explained that Asha Dan means "Gift of Hope." *"The poorest will be in a place to receive love and find hope because of your gift,"* Mother said. Then she talked happily about death, setting forth the vision of death as going home to an always loving Father. The woman thanked Mother Teresa for comforting her by removing some of her fear.

Share with Your Sufferings and Prayers. *"Why not become spiritually bound to the Missionaries of Charity whom you love? While we work in the slums, you share in the merit, the prayers and the work with your sufferings and prayers. I need souls like yours to pray and suffer for the work."*

This was Mother Teresa's invitation to Jacqueline de Decker in Belgium. Jacqueline had met Mother Teresa in 1948 as the new congregation was being founded. Her dream of joining Mother Teresa was crushed when, on her return to Belgium, Jacqueline underwent the first of many operations on her spine.

Mother Teresa wrote that Jacqueline would be a true Missionary of Charity, *"in body, in Belgium, but in soul, in India."* At Mother Teresa's request, Jacqueline became the link for Sick and Suffering Co-Workers.

In 1953 Mother Teresa sent her the names of the first twenty-seven novices to be linked with sick and suffering persons. Jacqueline linked the crippled and incurably sick people with the growing number of Missionaries of Charity. They exchanged letters once or twice a year. Eventually, thousands of Sick and Suffering Co-Workers around the world were linked in prayer with the Sisters, sharing Mother Teresa's vision: *"Suffering itself may be nothing, but suffering shared with Christ's passion is a wonderful gift."*

Jacqueline de Decker had to undergo over twenty agonizing operations, but she continues her work of putting the homebound and suffering in touch with Sisters in the farthest corners of a world in need. When she went to Co-Workers meetings, her body was encased in a steel brace, and she walked with steel crutches.

"You are a burning light which is being consumed for souls," Mother Teresa told her.

Mother Teresa had clothed a mysterious concept, that of the redemptive power of innocent suffering, in a personalized and concrete program of participating in a worldwide work of mercy—a call to mourn with those in pain so their sorrow can be turned into joy. She wrote to her Sick and Suffering Co-Workers, those who were daily bearing the cross: *"How happy I am to have you all. Often when the work is very hard, I think of*

51

you and tell God—'Look at my suffering children, and for their love—bless this work.' "

To another, she wrote, *"In reality, you can do much more on your bed of pain, than I, running on my feet, but you and I can do 'all things in Him who strengthens us.' "*

Mother Teresa in a moment of prayer.

Blessed are
the meek,
for they
shall inherit
the earth.

THREE

Blessed Are the Meek

WORDS TO PONDER

Blessed are the meek, for they shall inherit the earth.
Mt 5:5

Other words for "meek" are lowly, or gentle. In a competitive world, these words hardly express prized qualities. The aim of Mother Teresa's Sisters, "to remain right on the ground," and never to desert the lowliest, is lived out with spectacular fidelity. This fidelity stops people short, and even stuns them.

To see young women hurrying to teach in some of the most

desolate slums, where open drains carry away human waste, and where patties of cow dung lie out to dry for fuel gives one pause. To see them leave a dawn to comfort and care for the dying, is enough to cause one to stop and ask, "Why?"

Their actions present a mystery which only the Gospel can clarify. Their actions, performed with alacrity and joy, are understood in the light of the Gospel. It is Jesus who told us "Take my yoke upon your shoulders and learn from me, for I am gentle and humble of heart. Your souls will find rest, for my yoke is easy, and my burden light" (Mt 11:29-30).

The promise given to the meek is, "They shall possess the land." Possessing the land meant much in the society of Jesus' time, since land was the basis not only of sustenance, but of position and wealth. The possession of land was the justification for bloodshed, then as throughout the ages.

Of course, there are times when faith falters. One becomes sad at the powerlessness of our small actions, lowly things, done for lowly people. Mother Teresa reminds us of this, saying: *"Do the small things with great love."*

She asks people to emulate Mary, whose task of bearing the Son of God was the greatest given to any human person. As she proclaimed the glory of God, Mary rejoiced that God had looked at the humility, the lowliness of his handmaid, in coming to "the help of Israel, his servant."

> Lord Jesus,
> We want to imitate you, who told us;
> "I am meek and humble of heart."
> We ask you, that day by day, you lead us in this path.
> We wish to bring you, dear Christ, to others,
> in your freedom, in your liberation.
> Help us overcome our impatience, our anger,
> our tendency to manipulate others.
> Help us daily to cultivate meekness, humility, non-violence.

MOTHER TERESA IN HER OWN WORDS

By the Rule, adopted in 1950 and revised in 1988, Mother Teresa's Sisters received guidance for the "privilege" of performing their humble works. Always emphasized is the distinct vocation of giving "whole-hearted and free service to Christ in the distressing disguise of the poor."

We consider it an honor and privilege to serve Christ in the distressing disguise of the poorest of the poor with our humble work, and we do it with deep gratitude and profound reverence in a spirit of fraternal sharing, convinced that in accepting our humble service they make our existence as Missionaries of Charity possible.

Christ calls us through His church to labor for the salvation and sanctification of the poorest of the poor all over the world and so to satiate the thirst of God, dying on the Cross, which is the thirst for our love and the love of souls by:

> *loving him wholeheartedly and freely in the poorest of the poor with whom He identified Himself, both in our communities and in the people we serve, and so make His presence in them known, loved and served by all;*

> *making reparation for sins of hatred, coldness, lack of concern and love for Him in the world today, in one another and in the people we serve.*

Service means an unceasing and wholehearted labor in making ourselves available to Jesus so that He may live, in and through us, His life of infinitely tender, compassionate and merciful love, for the spiritually and materially poorest of the poor."

—From the Rule of the Missionaries of Charity

LIVING THE BEATITUDES

Having received permission, Mother Teresa put on a sari and stepped into the abyss of a new life on the streets of Calcutta. She started "right on the ground." She went to a "bustee," a slum community in Moti Jihl, where the children had no schools. She gathered some near-naked children around her, and borrowed a chair.

She sat near a tree and the children sat on the dusty earth. Starting with the alphabet, she used a stick to draw the letters on the ground, and had the children repeat them after her. Once they were familiar with the alphabet, the children were ready for the next step, reciting by rote from oilcloth posters.

From December 1948 to March 19, 1949, Mother Teresa's loneliness was intense. For twenty years, she had enjoyed the close association of the beloved community of the Loreto Sisters. Yet she persevered, traveling alone across Calcutta to one of the most pitiful slums of all. Moti Jihl meant Pearl Lake, so named from a small body of water in the center. It resembled a pearl—only if one pictured a black pearl, since its water was grimy, sump water.

By Easter 1949, two of her former students at St. Mary's School had joined Mother Teresa. They, too, adopted the simple cotton sari, thus identifying themselves with Calcutta's poorest. Sister Agnes and Sister Gertrude made it possible to gather more children, to give them the only education they would be likely to get.

Mother Teresa soon rented rooms among the poor of Moti Jihl, so that the classes could continue during the monsoons which lash Calcutta. This was the first of the humble slum schools founded by Mother Teresa. The word "humble" comes from *humilis*, whose root is *humus*, the earth, the ground. Mother Teresa placed her Sisters on the very ground of earth. Their formation rested on this commitment, as expressed in their Constitution.

In an early draft of the Rule, Mother Teresa said simply that *"following the lowliness of Christ, we shall remain right on the ground:*

by living Christ's concern for the poorest and the lowliest;

by being of immediate but effective service to them in all their needs, material and spiritual, until they can find some others who can help them in a better and more lasting way."

The Sisters were to be ready to give up the work as soon as others were ready to take it up.

Always Close to the Lowliest. "The Village of Widows," in Modhomgram, near Dacca, could not have been more desolate. During the conflict of 1971 that eventually led to the emergence of Bangladesh as an independent nation, invading soldiers killed all the men they encountered. All the men in Modhomgram were killed. The Missionaries of Charity adopted the Hindu village in predominantly Muslim Bangladesh. Sister Vincent, an outgoing Bengali, took me to visit Chopola in 1972. Chopola was the mother of nine children, and her daughter Nobadurga was the mother of several small children. They saw their husbands shot to death less than a year earlier.

Women like these had no way of making their living. They were the poorest of all, illiterate villagers, unskilled except in caring for their families. Sister Vincent, always close to the lowliest, knew that all Bengali village women could make puffed rice, a food used at breakfast and at other meals. The Sisters provided the rice; the widows prepared puffed rice on their little mud bucket stoves. They sold the prepared rice in the Dacca market.

The widows were soon making a popular candy (muri kadu) by adding date juice to the puffed rice. They sold these candies from a rented market stall in Dacca. Such practical projects, sponsored by the Sisters, kept these widows from becoming beggars on the city streets.

A sad note must be added to this account. A few years later, the happy, ebullient Bengali, Sister Vincent, was killed instantly in a traffic accident.

Meek and Humble of Heart. When the tiny band of Sisters led by Mother Teresa reached a dozen, it was accepted as a diocesan congregation, to work only in the diocese of Calcutta. The date was October 7, 1950, the Feast of Our Lady of the Rosary. The Decree of Praise that was then developed for members of the order included the fourth vow of "free and wholehearted service to the poorest of the poor." This vow would bind the new congregation to those thrown away and often forgotten by society, to the very "least of the brethren." After the Mass on October 7, in the upper room of an old Calcutta house, Sister Teresa, the school headmistress, became Mother Teresa. The guidelines for the Missionaries of Charity were read aloud. They included the following:

> *To fulfill our mission of compassion and love to the poorest of the poor we go*
> • *seeking out in towns and villages all over the world even amid*

*squalid surroundings, the poorest, the abandoned, the sick, the
infirm, the leprosy patients, the desperate, the lost, the outcasts,*

- *taking care of them,*
- *rendering help to them,*
- *visiting them assiduously,*
- *living Christ's love for them, and*
- *awakening their response to his great love.*

The patroness of the Missionaries of Charity is the Immaculate Heart of Mary. On the day of the feast, the Sisters join
in renewing their vows. Mother Teresa reminds her Sisters, as
she reminds her hearers in talks around the world, of the need
to make the humility of Mary our own.

To the immense crowd at the Eucharistic Congress in Philadelphia in 1976, she said, "*When his followers deserted Jesus, it
was Mary who stayed with him. She remained when He was spat
upon, treated like a leper, disowned by all and crucified.*

*Do we remain with our people when they are disowned, thrown
out, when they suffer? Do we give them our understanding love? Do
we have the eyes of compassion of Mary? Do we understand their
pain? Do we recognize their suffering?*

Mother Teresa appeals for the rights of the poor in Calcutta.

Blessed
are those who
hunger and thirst
for righteousness,
for they
shall be
satisfied.

FOUR

Blessed Are Those Who Hunger and Thirst for Righteousness

WORDS TO PONDER

Blessed are those who hunger and thirst for righteousness, for they shall be satisfied. **Mt 5:6**

Blessed are those who hunger and thirst after holiness. Both interpretations are valid: the inward, gnawing hunger for holiness and the thirst for it which nothing worldly can quench; as well as the longing for the outward achievement of justice.

How many revolutions have been declared to do away with

inequality and to establish justice once and for all? Rivers of blood have been shed when outrage and anger have spilled over into violence. History has shown that violence leads only to more violence and to greater oppression. Mother Teresa leads in a revolution of love.

A revolution of love takes more time than a bloody revolution to assume power, but it is one that lasts, one that does not leave victims in its wake.

Our thirst for justice, for holiness, can be nourished by the "living water" promised by Jesus (Jn 4:10).

In talking with the Samaritan woman, to whom he announced that he was the Messiah, Jesus promised her and all his followers that "living water."

In her talks, Mother Teresa keeps repeating: *Jesus made himself the Bread of Life to satisfy our hunger for God and for his love.*

The central act of the day for all Missionaries of Charity is the partaking of the Bread of Life at the Mass. It is at the table of the Lord that they find the strength to meet the hungers of the people they serve—

hunger for food when they are starving,
hunger for consolation when they are forsaken,

hunger for respect when they are humiliated,
hunger for a loving word when they are despised,
hunger for a smile when they are downcast.
Lord Jesus,
Help us to find a time each day,
if only for a few minutes,
to be close to you.
Teach us to pray as we ought
so that filled with your Spirit
we may reach out to the hunger
of those around us.

MOTHER TERESA IN HER OWN WORDS

Service must come from a heart filled with God.

To bring Christ to others depends on how we do what we do for the poor. We could do it one way, or we could do it some other way. I will never forget the time when a certain man visited our home for the poor who are dying. He arrived just as the Sisters were bringing in some of the dying off the streets. They had picked a man out of the gutter, and he was covered with worms. Without knowing she was being watched, a Sister came to care for the dying man. The visitor kept watching the Sister work. He saw how tenderly she cared for her patient. He noticed how tenderly she washed the man and smiled at him. She did not miss a detail in her attentive care for that dying man. I was also at the Home for the Dying that day.

The visitor, after carefully watching the Sister, turned to me and said, "I came here today, not believing in God, with my heart full of hate, but now I am leaving here believing in God. I have seen the love of God in action. Through the hands of that Sister—through her gestures, through her tenderness—which were so full of love for that wretched man, I have seen God's love descend upon him. Now I believe." I didn't even know who this visitor was at the time, or that he was an atheist.

This is what I expect from our Co-Workers. Do you want to do the same thing for those around you? You need to be united to Christ. You need prayer. Your service must come from a heart filled with God. —From a talk in London's Oratory, June 13, 1977

LIVING THE BEATITUDES

When Mother Teresa brought a team of Sisters to Lima, Peru, they settled in a deserted former motherhouse in a turbulent sector of the city called La Parada. They called their home, *Hogar de la Paz* (Home of Peace).

Behind its walls which enclosed a rectangular compound, there was order and peace. Reaching right up to the walls were some of the innumerable stands and stalls that extended for half a mile. Everything imaginable was being sold, new and used, in what people referred to as the "Thieves Market." Smoke rose from tiny food stalls feeding the teeming population in the market. Co-Workers, including men and women from many walks of life, doctors, teachers, housewives, and handymen, were soon enthusiastically volunteering at the Home of Peace.

One small group, however, did not welcome the Sisters, and stunned them by suggesting it would be better if they left. They were members of the clergy. They told the Sisters that the problems of Peru demanded more than the Sisters could give. It was time to change the very structures that gave rise to the poverty surrounding them.

The Missionaries of Charity were doing nothing to change these structures, they were told, and thus were prolonging the misery of the people. The critics expressed their hunger and thirst for justice in denouncing a system riddled with injustice. They wanted a complete turnover; any interim, small improvements, only delayed the downfall of evil structures.

Dom Helder Camara had addressed this issue when he shared the platform with Mother Teresa before eight thousand persons at the Eucharistic Congress in Philadelphia in 1976. Dom Helder talked of institutional violence and the need to build new structures. He stressed the nonviolence of Martin Luther King in changing society. There were those, he said, who felt that building the new structure was the only task, and that helping the poor could wait.

"But in the meantime—in the meantime," he said, looking toward Mother Teresa, "the hunger of the poor cries out for those who will feed and help them."

The Sisters in Lima did not reply. They were too busy with the backbreaking task of washing a rheumy-eyed old drunk left to die in the street, or of lifting sick children from their beds to change the bed clothes.

The gatekeeper of the Home of Peace had a name that pleased Mother Teresa immensely. He was called Jesus.

In bringing justice to those failed by society, Mother Teresa points to the new life made possible by changed relationships, between the rich and the merely comfortable, and the poorest of the poor; between those who have some power over their own lives and the lives of others, and those who are powerless.

As for the changing of structures, Mother Teresa said: *"Those who believe in changing structures may follow their consciences. Our work is with the individual person, with the poorest of the poor. Only by being one with us, has Jesus redeemed us. We are allowed to do the same; all the desolation of the poor people, not only their material poverty, but their spiritual destitution, must be redeemed."*

A Revolution of Hope. A young man meeting Mother Teresa in a side street in Calcutta knelt down to touch her feet. When Mother Teresa raised him up, he spoke very happily about his special day. This day he was getting married. He had been a beggar, close to death, and had been carried to the Home for the Dying. After being nursed back to life, the Sisters set him up in the business of shining shoes. This self-respecting citizen was now able to marry and set up a home. A revolution of hope had been achieved, one small life rescued from dying in the gutter. Mother Teresa's happiness was buoyant, for what she always wanted and worked for, was to give a needy human being strength and dignity.

Pedro's Goodness a Blessing. The story of one of the patients at Gift of Peace, the home for AIDS sufferers in Washington, D.C., was recounted by a Sister:

Pedro's family telephoned to ask if their twenty-five-year-old son could come to the Gift of Peace. They said he was not an easy character to help. Yet from the beginning, in June 1987, by the grace of God, he was the peacemaker among the men.

If someone was having a hard moment, he could find the right words to bring peace. He was very generous and kind to the others and showed real concern for them. He longed to make others happy by an encouraging word or a beautiful smile.

Pedro was Catholic and received the sacraments while at Gift of Peace. When he first came, his complaint to God was, that now that he had finished his studies, he could not pay back his educational loans. But he passed over this concern and soon established himself in practicing love and charity toward all. As time passed, his pain increased and he grew weaker. Yet he never complained and was patient with all who cared for him.

His parents came to be with him in his last days. They showed their deep love for him, as did his wife, who was with him daily. He was always fully conscious and never failed to give a smile to all. He died after a few months at

Gift of Peace. His goodness was a blessing. (The young man's real name was not Pedro.)

Small Programs But Beautiful. The longing of the victims of leprosy is to be productive in society like other citizens. Their hunger and thirst for the justice of participating in society, denied them by their affliction, is answered by work.

The practicality of the Missionaries is notable. The Brothers, caring for lepers at Gandhi's "Abode of Love" near Calcutta, help in their rehabilitation by supplying meaningful work.

The lepers make charpoys (the Indian bed resembling a hammock), and are trained to make sandals out of used automobile tires. They have looms on which they weave bedsheets and the blue-bordered saris worn by the Sisters. They are proud to make their own clothes. Some even manage to do some carpentry.

The Sisters reach out to street people in self-help programs involving the use of coconut shells. These are discarded by the thousands everyday in Calcutta. An army of poor people strip away the rough fibers, turning that material into coconut matting and rugs. What is left, the shells themselves, are then sold and used as fuel.

The simple hunger of lepers to take part in normal activities is answered, as is the desire of street people for work. That allows them to meet at least some of their own needs.

The gnawing feeling of isolation, suffered by the lepers and the very poor, is broken by these programs—small programs but beautiful in their effects on people.

Mother Teresa cradles a sick child at the Home for Dying Destitutes in Calcutta.

Blessed are
the merciful,
for they
shall obtain
mercy.

FIVE

Blessed Are the Merciful

WORDS TO PONDER

Blessed are the merciful, for they shall obtain mercy.

Mt 5:7

Mercy is more than a feeling of pity or compassion; mercy has to be expressed. It needs constant emphasis that mercy is love expressed under the aspect of need. Mercy is love going out to meet the need of the person loved. Mercy is prayer to the Father of all mercies on behalf of all who suffer.

Mother Teresa is a shining light in reminding the followers of Jesus of the implications of the parable of the Last Judgment. In it, Jesus assumed the personhood of the hungry one, the thirsty one, the naked and homeless one, the suffering and imprisoned one (Mt 25:35-40).

To those who reached out to him in mercy, he said, "You did it for me" (Mt 25:40). Here is the very core of Gospel living.

One of Mother Teresa's favorite gestures in talking of this parable is to take the forefinger of her right hand and point to each finger of her left hand. She repeats the words of Jesus, "You did it to me." Her work-worn, gnarled hands, which bring merciful care to many, tell their own tale.

Linked with the corporal works of mercy are the spiritual works of mercy:

> admonish the sinner,
> instruct the ignorant,
> counsel the doubtful,
> comfort the sorrowful,
> bear wrongs patiently,
> forgive injuries,
> pray for the living and the dead.

Those dedicated to the corporal works of mercy cannot help but be involved in the spiritual works of mercy.

Lord Jesus,
in your life you asked us
to be merciful, as our heavenly Father is merciful.
Mary assured us that
"His mercy is from age to age."
We ask that through the power of the Holy Spirit
we may grow daily in showing mercy.
We hope to obtain, despite our faults and failures,
the mercy which is the promise of this beatitude.

MOTHER TERESA IN HER OWN WORDS

Before a group of priests, Mother Teresa spoke on "You did it for me" (Mt 25:35-40).

When St. Paul was going to destroy the Christians in Damascus, he was thrown down and he heard the voice: "Saul, Saul, why dost thou persecute Me?" And He gave him a very clear answer: "I am Jesus Christ whom thou persecutest" (Acts 9:4-5).
"Whatever you do to the least of My brethren, you do to Me"

(Mt 25:40). If in My name, you give a glass of water, you give it to Me. If in My name, you receive a child, you receive Me (Mk 9:37).

He has made that as a condition also, that at the hour of death we are going to be judged on what we have been and what we have done. He makes Himself the hungry one, the naked one, the homeless one, the sick one, the lonely one, the unwanted one, the rejected one.

He says: "I was hungry and you gave Me to eat." Not only for bread, I was hungry for love. I was naked, not only for a piece of cloth, but I was naked for that human dignity of a child of God. I was homeless, not only for a home made of brick, but I was homeless, rejected, unwanted, unloved, a throw-away of society, and you did it to Me." Jesus in the Eucharist made Himself Bread of Life to satisfy our hunger for God, for we have all been created to love and to be loved.

It is very clear what Jesus meant, because how do we love God? If we have been created to love, we all want to love God, but how? Where is God? God is everywhere. How do we love God? And therefore, He gives us the opportunity to do to others what we would like to do to Him, to put our love for Him in a living action.

Mother Teresa, in the Rule, describes the work of the Sisters:

loving and serving Him in the distressing disguise of the poorest of the poor, both materially and spiritually, recognizing in them and restoring to them the image and likeness of God.
They fulfill the Rule

- *by nursing the sick and dying destitutes;*
- *by gathering and teaching the poor and little street children;*
- *by giving shelter to the abandoned and homeless;*
- *by caring for the unwanted, the unloved and the lonely;*
- *by going out to the spiritually poorest of the poor to proclaim the Word of God by our presence and spiritual works of mercy.*

LIVING THE BEATITUDES

After she had begun to work among slum children, Mother Teresa found she had to pass dying men, women, and even children on the streets of the refugee-swollen city.

This was Mother Teresa's response to seeing the image of God perishing in filth and spittle.

Mother Teresa said of those days, "*I could not allow children of God to die like animals in the gutter."* When she received a few rupees, she importuned taxi drivers to drive her and the helpless scraps of humanity to local hospitals.

One day when she borrowed a wheelbarrow to trundle a suffering ragged man to a hospital, Mother Teresa and her patient were turned away. The Home for the Dying in Calcutta might be said to have grown from a wheelbarrow.

Mother Teresa refused to leave, standing her ground on behalf of the agonizing person. He was finally admitted to the hospital.

Some persons at the point of death were not being accepted anywhere. For them, Mother Teresa rented two dirt-floored rooms in the Moti Jihl slum. There she, with the Sisters, cared for dying men, women, and children until they recovered sufficiently to return to the streets, or until they passed through the doors of death.

"At least," Mother Teresa said, *"I can give them a human death."* It was all she could do to validate the inviolable dignity of the human person.

A Blessing from God through an Act of Mercy. The mercy shown by Mother Teresa and the Missionaries of Charity in

Calcutta aroused marvelous echoes among the vastly differing religious groups that make up the city.

One of Mother Teresa's parable-like tales of a newlywed Hindu couple is a poignant example of how two young people expressed their love, by sacrificing pomp and luxury in favor of mercy for the hungry.

A beautiful thing happened in Calcutta. Two young people came to see me, Hindu people. They gave me a very big amount of money. "How did you get so much money?" I asked them. They answered me, "We got married two days ago. Before our marriage, we decided we would not have a big wedding feast, and we would not buy wedding clothes. We decided we would give the money we saved to you to feed the people."

In a big Hindu family, a rich family, it is a scandal not to have special wedding clothes and not to have a wedding feast. "Why did you do that?" I asked them. And they answered me, "Mother, we love each other so much that we wanted to obtain a special blessing from God by making a sacrifice. We wanted to give each other this special gift."

Isn't that beautiful? Things like that are happening every day, really beautiful things. We must pull them out. We have to pull out the wonderful things that are happening in the world."

Our People. A happy moment in the life of Mother Teresa occurred after she had come with the first four Sisters to work in Mexico City. Sister Frederick, who spoke Spanish, was asking the people of a poor area about their needs. "La Palabra de Dios" (The Word of God) came the reply from some poor families. Mother Teresa's eyes were alight with joy. Whenever the Sisters were asked, they were ready with lessons in the Gospel and in preparation for the sacraments.

The place chosen by the Sisters for their work was a vast garbage dump on the edge of Mexico City, perhaps the most populous city of the world. Here thousands of tons of refuse were thrown every day; here the poorest of Mexico's millions made their home. "These are our people," the Sisters said.

The people worked diligently, sorting through the *basura* (garbage), for any usable articles, bottles, broomsticks, cans, and pieces of furniture. Buyers came in trucks every day, to deal with the garbage sorters. The community living in the *basura* keeps pigs, goats, and chickens. They use the pesos they earn to add beans and tortillas to their diet.

With the help of the President of Mexico, a plot of land was given to the Sisters. With help from many sources, a home for the dying and the abandoned was built near the garbage dump, then a clinic staffed by volunteer doctors, and finally, a home for abandoned children. These little ones had many handicaps: some were blind, some had deformed limbs, some had cleft palates and some had bodies shrunken from hunger. Co-Workers quickly gathered round the Sisters to bring the children to as much normalcy as their handicaps would permit.

"Our people," for the Missionaries of Charity, were also the garbage-pickers of Cairo, Egypt. Out beyond the City of the Dead, the expanse of tombs around which many of the living make their homes, is the dumping-ground for Cairo's refuse.

An array of over ten thousand garbage-collectors go out in donkey carts to gather the refuse; therefore, they have the privilege of sorting it for saleable objects. Their entire life and livelihood is based on garbage, as one can see by the pigs around their huts, pigs kept alive by rooting in the garbage.

In one corner of the dumping-ground are the dispensary and welfare center of the Missionaries of Charity. Among the members of this deprived community, mainly Christian, family life is strong. The men and younger people command the donkey carts, with the loading and the unloading. The nimble fingers of the women pick out tins, pieces of material, even parts of cheap jewelry.

Sister Valerie from Malta and five other Sisters run a busy dispensary for wheezing and crying children. The women come to the classes to learn the basics of sewing and other crafts, as well as hygiene. (Hygiene classes involve supplies of precious soap.)

Mother Teresa in a moment of quiet reflection.

Blessed are
the pure
in heart,
for they
shall see
God.

Blessed Are
the Pure in Heart

WORDS TO PONDER

Blessed are the pure in heart, for they shall see God. **Mt 5:8**

"Clean of heart" is also given as "pure in heart" or "single-hearted." In Scripture, the heart includes not only the emotions, but the mind and the will—in fact, the whole person.

Being clean of heart, pure, and single-hearted images the whole person turned toward God, forsaking all lesser goods. Purity of heart means simply to will one thing. An old phrase, used less today, "the one thing necessary," is apt here. The one thing necessary is salvation, union with God forever.

The clean of heart move through life constantly choosing God, so that as they leave life, they receive the promise of this Beatitude: they enter the presence of the Creator. The clean of heart, however, do not have to pass from the earth to have a vision of the divine.

They see the Spirit of God in those close to them, in their friends, and in the people they meet on life's pilgrimage. As followers of Jesus, those who strive to be single-hearted can glimpse the Spirit of God in their opponents, even in those who may hate them and wish them evil.

St. Augustine pointed out that God "made his Son not only show the way but to be the very Way Himself."

Jesus as the very Way is the way of the single-hearted, concentrating on doing the will of God. This implies a certain emptying of the self, a discarding of what does not lead to God. We remember that Jesus "emptied himself, and took the form of a slave" in obedience to the Father (Phil 2:7).

Those of us fortunate enough to know Mother Teresa marvel at this quality in her. She seems to be an empty reed through which the Spirit blows. With her heart and mind intent on God, she is free to carry out his will in serving his creatures with gladness.

As the number of houses of the Missionaries of Charity has

grown in number, and the Sisters have worked in a troubled world, Mother Teresa has not wasted her energy in anxiety and fear. Her energies continue to be poured out in an exhausting schedule of travel for visitations and talks.

She prays, dismissing all anxiety from her mind, carrying out St. Paul's teaching: "Dismiss all anxiety from your minds. Present your needs to God in every form of prayer and in petitions full of gratitude. Then God's own peace, which is beyond all understanding, will stand guard over your hearts and minds, in Christ Jesus" (Phil 4:6-7).

When some young people asked Mother Teresa how they could learn to see and serve Jesus in the poor, she replied, *"You need a clean heart."*

"In our life of prayer," Mother Teresa tells her Sisters in the Rule of the Order, *"great freedom and openness to the movement of the Spirit, spontaneity and creativity will be encouraged."*

The Sisters, like Mother Teresa, do not seem to have needs of their own. Their whole attention is apparently on God, and on the needs of those they serve in his name. The Sisters follow Mother Teresa in seeing what others may fail to see, as they reach out with the spiritual works of mercy in special ways.

Lord Jesus,
we want to be pure of heart
and we desire the reward—seeing you—
now, in your children, of all peoples and beliefs,
and later, in your kingdom.
Make us open to the Holy Spirit,
that we may will one thing, the salvation of all,
including those we serve and ourselves.

MOTHER TERESA IN HER OWN WORDS

Let us thank God for His great love in bringing us together to realize the greatness of His love for each one of us, for none of us would be here if the good God did not put that love—that tender love—in the heart of our mother; to keep us, to give us love, to give us joy of living and loving. That is why it is good for a few seconds that we just thank our mother for giving us the joy of living and loving.

We all also owe a deep gratitude to Mary the mother of Jesus, for accepting to be the mother of Christ; for accepting to bear Him for nine months, for accepting to take care of Him, to love Him, to protect Him.

That's why we'll ask her to give us her heart—so beautiful, so pure, so immaculate—her heart so full of love and humility, that we may also be able to receive Jesus the Bread of Life, as she received Him. To love Him as she loved Him, and to serve Him in the distress and disguise of the poorest of the poor.

We read in the Gospel that God loved the world so much that He gave Jesus to the most pure virgin, Mary. And she, on receiving Jesus, went in haste to her cousin's home to Elizabeth, who was "with child."

And something very strange happened when she came there: the little unborn child in the womb of Elizabeth "leaped with joy" at the presence of Jesus. Very strange: that God used an unborn child to proclaim the coming of Christ.

And we know today what terrible things are happening to that little unborn child. The mother herself kills, destroys, murders her own child with her own decision.

So I think it is good for one second we pray: "God have mercy on them."

I have met many mothers who have done this: who have killed their own child, but that child is a child. It is a living presence of God created for greater things: to love and to be loved. And that child is somebody special to God.

—Talk by Mother Teresa given to the Commissioners prior to

Closeness to God. Precious counsels from the Rule of the Missionaries of Charity have much to say to lay people struggling for closeness to God in a world of relentless competitiveness, endless distractions, and unbridled consumerism. Mother Teresa says:

> *We are called in a very special way on behalf of the poorest of the poor to remain immersed together with Mary in the contemplation of the Father, Son and the Holy Spirit, in their love for one another as well as in their love for us, manifested in the great marvels of creation, redemption and sanctification.*
>
> *We need silence to be alone with God, to speak to Him, to listen to Him, to ponder His words deep in our hearts. We need to be alone with God in silence to be renewed and to be transformed. Silence gives us a new outlook on life. In it we are filled with the energy of God Himself that makes us do all things with joy.*
>
> *God is the friend of silence. His language is "Be still and know that I am God" (Ps 46:10). He requires us to be silent to discover Him. In the silence of the heart God speaks.*

—From the Rule of the Missionaries of Charity

LIVING THE BEATITUDES

Being clean of heart or single-hearted means that one cannot be deflected from the path to God, from doing his will.

In her single-hearted defense of the sacredness of life, Mother Teresa moves hearts and minds as few others. After her defense of life to the Commissioners, prior to the 200th General Assembly of the Presbyterian Church, a woman was asked by a reporter for her reaction.

The woman burst into tears as she told him that she was going to have to rethink the whole matter of abortion.

Another church commissioner wrote:

> I must admit that I have been somewhat of a fence sitter. No longer.... The highlight was hearing Mother Teresa. It was a deeply moving experience for me, and I am not the same as a result. Her message, along with the witness of Presbyterians Pro-Life, has left a mark on my life.

Mother Teresa's clear vision pierces the hesitancy, even confusion, of men and women anxiously searching for an answer to the moral dilemma of terminating life in the womb.

Even those who reach a different conclusion from Mother

Teresa on the abortion issue, respect the witness of her life which undergirds the witness of her words. She explains, *"In Calcutta, we send word to the clinics, the police stations and the hospitals: Please do not destroy the child. I will take the child. So our house is always full of children."*

"There is a joke in Calcutta," she relates, *"about Mother Teresa —that she is always talking about natural family planning and abortion, but everyday she has more and more children."*

She explains that in India, the many adoptions from the Children's Home (Shishu Bhavam) are near-miracles. Caste barriers fall as Indian families take as their own, little ones who might not have been allowed to be born.

Living in the Presence. Here is another response to her talk:

"Somehow Mother Teresa fails to understand how complicated life is on this planet," wrote the Reverend Bart Tarman in the *Presbyterian Pro-Life News*. "She thinks it's simple: 'to love and be loved.' Doesn't she know about famine, disease, war, poverty, senility, deformity, hunger, and death? Wrong question—she lives closer to calamities than any of us. How then can she be so close to the complexities of evil and believe in simplicity, so close to hate and believe in love, so close to ugliness and believe in beauty?"

In the words of the Quaker, Thomas Kelly, she has found the secret of "living in the Presence." When you are with her, you sense she is truly there for you—there all the way. Yet on a quieter, deeper, subterranean level of the soul you also sense that she is with Another... and she is completely His.

Many people who meet her are struck by the radiant joy in her face. As one priest said to me before I met her, "She isn't pretty, but she sure is beautiful!"

But I was captured by her hands. Whenever she met anyone, she held out her hands together—fingertips touching, palms slightly apart—in a prayer-like gesture, raising them up while she herself bowed down. To me it seemed a gesture of respect, reminding her (and perhaps the other as well) that she was in the presence of Christ through this simple encounter with another human being. Here was "the image of God" in the person before her.

All the time she spoke with another person, her aged, character-ridden hands (hands which have picked up thousands beggars from the gutters) were caressing Rosary beads, as she prayed somewhere in the recesses of her heart in the very presence of Christ. Paul's admonition to pray without ceasing took on literal meaning for the first time in my life.

Over and over again in many different contexts she said, *"It's so simple, no?"* that you found yourself answering "Yes" and for a fleeting second, actually believing it.

What does she say about abortion and the unborn? *"It's so simple. The unborn child was created by God to love and be loved. If you don't want the child, give him to me. I want him."* Simple, no?

She seems constantly aware of the presence of God. She seems to be in continuous communion with Him at a deep level of her being. She seems aware of His presence (if only through creation), in everyone around her. And most of all, she really seems to believe what Jesus taught!

—From 200th General Assembly, Commissioners of the Presbyterian Church (USA), June 1988 (Reprinted with permission.)

Mother Teresa on the streets of Belfast in Northern Ireland.

Blessed are
the peacemakers,
for they
shall be called
children
of God.

SEVEN

Blessed Are the Peacemakers

WORDS TO PONDER

Blessed are the peacemakers, for they shall be called children of God. **Mt 5:9**

When Mother Teresa arrived to visit her Sisters in East Beirut, she found herself in the midst of war's devastation.

"*I have never been in a war before,*" she remarked, "*but I have seen famine and death. I was asking myself what do they feel when they do this. I don't understand it. They are all children of God. Why do they do it? I don't understand.*"

While never in an actual war, Mother Teresa had known death by violence in Calcutta. She had seen the results of the days of the Great Killing, when Muslim and Hindu had risen against each other. The episode resulted in the deaths of over five thousand, and the injuries of uncounted thousands.

Her work on the agonized streets of Calcutta rose out of such violence and suffering.

Modern wars, through bombing and long-distance shelling, find their chief targets in noncombatants, the innocent inhabitants of cities near targeted military installations. For this reason, the world's bishops at the Second Vatican Council, condemned indiscriminate warfare as "a crime against God and man himself."

What Mother Teresa could not understand was the taking of life.

I think that no human hand should be raised to kill life, since life is God's gift to us, even in an unborn child. And I think that the cry of these children who are killed before coming into the world must be heard by God. Life is God's greatest gift to human beings, and humans are created in the image of God. Life belongs to God, and we do not have the right to destroy it. War is the killing of human beings. How can this be just?

The Norwegian Nobel Committee explained that the choice of Mother Teresa for the Nobel Peace Prize served "to remind the world of the words spoken by Fridjof Nansen: 'Love of one's neighbor is realistic policy.'"

The promise held out to peacemakers in this Beatitude is nothing less than to be called "children of God."

Would anyone want to be other than a child of God?

Mother Teresa helps us toward the realization of this goal on our earthly pilgrimage.

Lord Jesus,
cleanse us of those personal failings
which diminish our own peace
and the peace of those around us.
Keep our minds and hearts serene
so we may bring peace to all we meet.
We want to witness to peace.
We ask that you will lead our violent world
to peace.

MOTHER TERESA IN HER OWN WORDS

The Christian has to learn to forgive, for the anger and hatred that cause wars and conflicts originate in the human heart. We must realize that, in order to be forgiven, we have to be able to forgive and let go of anger and grudges against others. Forgiveness offers us a clean heart, and people will be a hundred times better after it.

In his passion Jesus taught us to forgive out of love, how to forget out of humility. So let us examine our hearts and see if there is any unforgiven hurt—any unforgotten bitterness!

The quickest and surest way is the "tongue"—use it for the good of others, if you think well of others. From the abundance of the heart the mouth speaketh. If your heart is full of love, you will speak of love.

It is easy to love those who are far away. It isn't always easy to love those who are right next to us. It is easier to offer a dish of rice to satisfy the hunger of a poor person, than to fill up the loneliness and suffering of someone lacking love in our own family.

—Talk to Co-Workers, unpublished

Works of Love, Works of Peace. On receiving the news of the Nobel Peace Prize in December of 1979, Mother Teresa said: *"I thank God for this great gift, and for making the world acknowledge works of love to be works of peace."*

As Mother Teresa regards life as God's greatest gift, she

made the protection of life the main theme of the Nobel acceptance speech.

This protection begins with the child in the womb and includes every member of the human family at every stage of life. Her peace message runs counter to the laws of many nations, and to the arms stockpiles targeted at this or that segment of humankind.

The Peace Award ceremony differed from that of other years. It began with prayer led by Mother Teresa. "The Peace Prayer of St. Francis" was distributed to all present in the great hall of the University of Oslo. Present were royalty, diplomats, politicians, members of the academy, and of the press.

Some words of Mother Teresa's acceptance speech for the Peace Prize follow:

As we have gathered here together to thank God for the Nobel Peace Prize, I think it will be beautiful that we pray the prayer of St. Francis of Assisi which always surprises me very much. We pray this prayer every day after Holy Communion, because it is very fitting for each one of us.

And I always wonder that over seven hundred years ago when St. Francis of Assisi composed this prayer, the world had the same difficulties that we have today. This prayer fits our situa-

tion very nicely. I think some of you already have got it—so we will pray together:

Lord, make me a channel of Thy peace
that where there is hatred, I may bring love;
that where there is wrong, I may bring the spirit of forgiveness;
that where there is discord, I may bring harmony;
that where there is error, I may bring truth;
that where there is doubt, I may bring faith;
that where there is despair, I may bring hope;
that where there are shadows, I may bring light;
that where there is sadness, I may bring joy.

Lord, grant that I may seek rather
to comfort than to be comforted,
to understand than to be understood,
to love than to be loved; for
it is by forgetting self that one finds;
it is by forgiving that one is forgiven;
it is by dying that one awakens to eternal life.
Amen.

Let us thank God for this gift of peace, that reminds us that we have been created to live that peace, and that Jesus became man to bring that good news to the poor. The good news was peace to all of good will, and this is something that we all want—peace of heart.

When the Virgin Mary discovered that He had come into her life, she went in haste to give that good news to her cousin, Elizabeth. The child in the womb of Elizabeth leaped with joy. That little unborn child recognized the Prince of Peace. He recognized that Christ had come to bring the good news, for you and for me.

Christ died on the Cross to show that greater love. He died for you and for me and for that leper, and for that man dying of hunger, and for that naked person lying in the streets, not only of Calcutta, but of Africa and New York, London and Oslo.

He insisted that we love one another, as He loves each of us. We read that in the Gospel. As the Father loved Him and He loved us, so we must love one another until it hurts. It is not enough for us to say, "I love God, but I do not love my neighbor." How can you love God, whom you do not see, if you do not love your neighbor whom you see, whom you touch, with whom you live?

— Acceptance Speech, Nobel Peace Prize, December 10, 1979

LIVING THE BEATITUDES

A follower of Gandhi living in London, Satish Kumar, had the dream of "A World Prayer For Peace." Kumar was soon joined by other peacemakers who shared with him a belief in "the transforming power of the shared word."

They trusted that believers of all Christian groups, as well as those faithful to other religious traditions—and including agnostics, humanistic, and free thinkers, too—would join in the peace prayer.

They decided to launch the prayer in London. They asserted that the launching event "could only have full meaning if the prayer were given authority of someone of manifest purity of heart." It was felt that it should be "someone whose life was a way of peace."

"The appropriate person would live in the most common thoroughfare of the world, that of the poor, and would demonstrably see, in the face of various teeming humanity, the single countenance of the Son of Peace."

Mother Teresa was chosen.

In the crowded Church of St. James in Piccadilly, in the heart of London, Mother Teresa recited the prayer.

Lead me from death to life,
from falsehood to truth;
lead me from despair to hope,
from fear to trust;
lead me from hate to love,

from war to peace;
let peace fill our hearts,
our world, our universe.
Peace.   Peace.   Peace.

Currently the prayer is in frequent use in classrooms, in peace meetings, and in meetings of different faith groups, as well as secular groups throughout the world. Mother Teresa commended the prayer to all Co-Worker groups.

The Fruit of Service Is Peace. This is the message on a little card given out by Mother Teresa. Smiling, she says, "*This is my business card,*" explaining that it was printed for her by a Hindu who supports her work.

The fruit of Silence is Prayer.
The fruit of Prayer is Faith.
The fruit of Faith is Love.
The fruit of Love is Service.
The fruit of Service is Peace.

Joining Pope John Paul II and religious leaders of many faiths, Mother Teresa made a personal appeal for peace to

President George Bush and President Saddam Hussein to avoid bloodshed in the Persian Gulf. Sadly, her appeal was not heeded. May it be our prayer in appealing to leaders of our nation and those of other nations who find themselves on the brink of armed conflict.

I come to you with tears in my eyes in God's love to plead for the poor, if the horror we all dread happens. I beg you to labor for God's peace and be reconciled with one another. In the short term, there may be winners and losers in a war, but that can never justify the suffering, pain and loss of life, which your weapons will cause.

I beg you to save our brothers and sisters, because they are given to us by God to love and to cherish.

—*Calcutta Herald*, January 11, 1991

Mother Teresa filled with the joy of the Lord.

Blessed are those
who are persecuted
for righteousness' sake,
for theirs is the kingdom of heaven.

Blessed are you
when men revile you
and persecute you
and utter all kinds of evil
against you falsely on my account.
Rejoice and be glad,
for your reward is great in heaven.

EIGHT

Blessed Are Those Who Suffer Persecution for Righteousness' Sake

WORDS TO PONDER

Blessed are those who are persecuted for righteousness' sake, for theirs is the kingdom of heaven. **Mt 5:10**

Blessed are you when men revile you and persecute you and utter all kinds of evil against you falsely on my account. Rejoice and be glad, for your reward is great in heaven.

Mt 5:11-12

"Mother Teresa's cross was the first sign of Christianity seen on our state television since at least 1967," stated a refugee from Albania as he arrived in Italy in 1990. The cross he referred to was the black cross on Mother Teresa's white sari.

While the Marxist regime persecuted believers (Catholics, Orthodox, and Muslims) from 1944 onward, the situation became worse after 1967. It was then that her native Albania officially declared itself an atheist nation, the only one on the face of the globe. The onslaught on religion became even more savage. The treatment of Catholics was a reminder of the persecution by the worst of the Roman emperors. In actuality, the church was driven into the catacombs.

It was strange indeed that, while Mother Teresa traversed the globe with the words of Jesus on her lips, and his works of mercy were multiplied by her hands, the name of Jesus could not be spoken publicly by the people of Albania.

An imprisoned parish priest was asked by a fellow prisoner to baptize his child. He did so in secret. When the authorities discovered the forbidden act, the priest was sentenced to death. He was one of sixty priests who perished either by hanging, by firing squad, or by the rigors of labor camps.

Persecution, as we all have learned, has been a mark of Christianity from the beginning. This Beatitude calls those who endure persecution "blessed" for upholding righteousness and the teachings of righteousness.

The promise that accompanies this Beatitude is a breathtaking one, no less than the possession of the kingdom of heaven.

Lord Jesus,
we know that to imitate you
we must work for the good of all people.
You have told us that we will suffer
as we make our feeble efforts for others,
    against oppression,
    against degradation,
    against war.
Daily we meet opposition, contradiction.
Help us accept our small sufferings,
for we know they have a redemptive power.
Turn our grief to joy
as we strive to extend your will.

MOTHER TERESA IN HER OWN WORDS

The Joy of the Risen Christ. One of Mother Teresa's repeated counsels is:

Never let anything so fill you with pain or sorrow so as to make you forget the joy of Christ Risen.

She reminds people during life's trials of the never-failing protestations of a loving God in Scripture and the importance of prayer and sacrifice in resisting persecution.

> I will not forget you....
> I have graven you on the palms of
> my hands.... I have called you by
> name.... You are mine.... You are precious
> to Me.... I love you.
> —Based on Is 49:16, Is 43:1,4

"Blessed are those who suffer persecution": To resist persecution, we need continual refilling of prayer and sacrifice—of the Bread of Life, of the Living Water, of our Sisters in community, and of the poor. We need Our Lady, our mother, to be with us always, to protect us and keep us only for Jesus.

Prayer enlarges the heart until it is capable of containing God's gift of Himself. Ask and seek and your heart will grow big enough to receive Him and keep Him as your own.

—Motherhouse, February 18, 1967

The Rule of the Missionaries of Charity offers much to people living in a world in which fear and suffering abound. She writes of the mystery of the Cross, as it provides meaning for suffering, and as a sign of the love of Jesus, our brother, who carried it for us all.

> *The Cross will be for us as it was for Christ: proof of the greatest love. Jesus alone, God made man, could fully understand the meaning of sin and suffer from it.*
>
> *The force with which Christ was drawn to His Cross, in expiation for the sin of mankind, must urge us as Spouses of Jesus Crucified to accept voluntary nailing with Christ on the Cross, in a spirit of love, obedience and reparation for our own sinfulness and that of the world, especially our poor.*

- *to fill up in our flesh what is lacking of the suffering of Christ on behalf of His Body, the Church;*
- *to express our union and sharing in the sufferings of our poor, for their salvation and sanctification;*
- *to give witness of penance so that the people of God will have the courage to accept it also in their own lives.*

—From the Rule of the Missionaries of Charity

LIVING THE BEATITUDES

Mother Teresa endured great hardship because of the Albanian government's harsh decrees: namely, forced separation from her mother and sister in Tirana. After leaving her home at eighteen, Mother Teresa never saw them again.

Mother Teresa's only brother, Lazar, living in Palermo, Sicily, was often asked about his well-known younger sister. On one occasion, he burst out,

Mother Teresa, I call her that now, is silent about the persecution she is suffering. She comes to Rome often. In a few hours she could be in Tirana, Albania, with her mother. Or, in a few hours, our mother could be in Italy—also our only sister, Age. I could take care of them, and my mother could see her only grandchildren. I cannot be silent about it.

As a widow, Mrs. Drana Bojaxhui had developed a textile and carpet business to support her three children. Profoundly religious, she attended Mass daily, and helped ailing neighbors, even nursing them in her own home. With her daughter Age, she left her home in Skopje, Yugoslavia, to settle in newly-freed Albania. From Tirana, she had written to Mother Teresa: "I want to see you before I die. That is the only grace I ask of God."

Mother Teresa's suffering on behalf of her mother and sister was intensified by the awareness of the cruel society in which they were forced to live. She maintained complete silence about her own pain.

After the death of her mother and sister, Mother Teresa wrote,

> *We will meet in heaven. Since I belong to Jesus, the people of the world are my people, and so the poor are my Brothers and Sisters. My mother and sister must be very happy to be home with God, and I am sure their love and prayers are always with me.*
>
> *When I go home to God, for death is nothing else but going home to God, the bond of love will be unbroken for all eternity.*

Her own cross was far lighter than the cross of those trapped inside Albania. Mother Teresa accepted the fact that over the years the Lord had allowed her to visit the poorest of the poor around the world, bringing them solace and comfort, while she was unable to visit the very woman who gave her life.

Struggle to Care for the Scorned. Persecution can come to the Christian in many ways, in trials that tempt us to desert the hard path of following Jesus for an easier one of accommodating to the way of the world. Mother Teresa was assailed by many such trials in the early months and years of her work among the poorest of the poor.

A good and generous Jesuit priest, who later became one of her strongest supporters, was aghast when he saw Mother Teresa in her new garb for the first time. The sedate teacher, in a flowing floor-length habit with traditional tight headdress, now appeared in a rough cotton sari held by a large safety pin. Her stockingless feet were shod with cheap sandals.

The nun who had remained behind the walls of a girls' school, now walked the streets of a city in turmoil. She was making her way to slums where open sewers ran between crowded huts, or community privies gave out a killing stench. His first reaction was to say, "I thought she was cracked."

Not all the people of Calcutta welcomed the work of Mother Teresa and the Missionaries of Charity. A group of students once came to the Home for the Dying with the intention of removing Mother Teresa from the scene. They objected to the presence of Mother Teresa and her Sisters in the heart of a Hindu shrine (the temple of Kali). They feared that she and her Sisters could turn good Hindus from their religion.

Their leader entered the Home for the Dying and confronted Mother Teresa. He also confronted the forsaken human creatures who were being fed, washed, and having their sores dressed.

He went out to his fellow-protesters, stating that he would assist in ejecting Mother Teresa and the Sisters on one condition. The condition was that they would enlist their own mothers and sisters to continue the work. The group broke up and left quietly.

"The miracle," Mother Teresa remarked of the Home for the Dying, *"is not that we do this work, but that we are happy to do it."*

Turning Points in Mother Teresa's Life

She was born on August 26, 1910, and baptized the following day in Skopje, Yugoslavia, where her family was part of the Albanian community.

♦ ♦ ♦

As a teenager, Agnes Gonxha Bojaxhia's heart was set on fire by accounts of the Catholic mission work in Bengal, India.

♦ ♦ ♦

At the age of eighteen, she entered the Loreto Sisters (Institute of the Blessed Virgin Mary), in Dublin, Ireland.

♦ ♦ ♦

On January 6, 1929 (Feast of the Epiphany), she arrived by ship in Calcutta, the capital of Bengal.

In 1931, she made her first vows as a Sister of Loreto, taking the name of a recently canonized saint, St. Thérèse of Lisieux. In 1937, she took lifetime vows of poverty, chastity, and obedience.

◆ ◆ ◆

Sister Teresa, a much-loved teacher and headmistress, lived through the wartime agony of Bengal, including the 1943 famine, and the upheaval of India's struggle for freedom.

◆ ◆ ◆

On September 10, 1946, Sister Teresa took the train to Darjeeling for her retreat. She relates: *"It was on that train that I heard the call to give up all and follow Him into the slums—to serve Him in the poorest of the poor. The message was quite clear. I was to leave the convent and work with the poor while living among them."*

◆ ◆ ◆

With permission from the Holy See, from Loreto, and from the Archbishop of Calcutta, Sister Teresa obeyed "the call within a call" by adopting the cheap sari of the poor, and going alone to a Calcutta slum.

◆ ◆ ◆

After a number of former students joined her, a new congregation was born: the Missionaries of Charity. The date was October 7, 1950. Sister Teresa became Mother Teresa, founder of a new order.

◆ ◆ ◆

The Rule of the Missionaries of Charity states: *"Our religious family started when our Foundress, Mother M. Teresa Bojaxhia, was inspired by the Holy Spirit with a special charism on the 10th of September, 1946. This inspiration or charism means that the Holy Spirit communicated God's will to Mother."*

◆ ◆ ◆

The Home for the Dying at Kalighat was opened in 1952.

◆ ◆ ◆

Mother Teresa, on her first trip outside of India, spoke at the National Assembly of the National Council of Catholic Women (Las Vegas, Nevada, 1960). A link of help was established between NCCW and the Missionaries of Charity through Catholic Relief Services, the overseas aid agency of the American Catholic community.

◆ ◆ ◆

The Missionary Brothers of Charity were founded in Calcutta in 1963 and soon had houses around the world.

The International Association of Co-Workers of Mother Teresa, already functioning unofficially for many years, was recognized in 1969 by Pope Paul VI as an affiliate of the Missionaries of Charity. Mrs. Ann Blaikie, a former resident of Calcutta, was the co-founder. Dr. Warren Kump and Mrs. Patricia Kump initiated the Co-Workers in the United States.

◆ ◆ ◆

Malcolm Muggeridge's book on Mother Teresa, *Something Beautiful for God*, appeared in 1971 and was translated into many languages.

◆ ◆ ◆

In 1976, the Contemplative Missionaries of Charity in New York City was formed; and in 1984, also in New York City, the Priest Missionaries of Charity was founded.

◆ ◆ ◆

Among the avalanche of honors that came to Mother Teresa was the 1979 Nobel Peace Prize, which, in a special way, carried the story of her work and its spirit around the world.

The Petrie Production film, "Mother Teresa," a much-praised documentary, brought the reality of the work to countless people through television and videotapes.

Throughout the last three decades, Mother Teresa has been able to respond to requests from church leaders, often supported by local civil authorities, to bring teams of Sisters to places of misery and need, in the farthest corners of the globe.

The Sisters pour out their lives in works of mercy in North America, the Carribean, Central and South America, in the Middle East, Africa, Asia, Australia, Oceania, and the European continent, including the Commonwealth of Independent States, formerly the Soviet Union.

◆ ◆ ◆

On a visit to China in 1985, Mother Teresa offered to bring the Sisters to work for the poor and disabled. The son of Deng Ziaoping, a leader of work for the disabled, and himself disabled, turned down the offer.

◆ ◆ ◆

In 1986, Mother Teresa experienced the "happiest day of my life" when she took Pope John Paul II to meet "her treasures" in the Home for the Dying in Calcutta.

◆ ◆ ◆

In 1988, Mother Teresa took teams of her Sisters to the then

Soviet Union. In 1990, the call to Siberia came, and in 1991, the long-awaited call to Albania came.

♦ ♦ ♦

In 1990, Mother Teresa was elected Mother General of the Missionaries of Charity for the duration of her lifetime.

♦ ♦ ♦

On a trip to Europe and North America in December of 1991, Mother Teresa's overtaxed heart began to fail and she was hospitalized in serious condition in La Jolla, California. Her health partially restored, she continued her trip on January 15, 1992.

♦ ♦ ♦

As of May, 1992, there are Sisters, Brothers, and Fathers of the Missionaries of Charity in five hundred houses located in ninety-seven countries. Mother Teresa prays fervently that soon members of her order will be allowed to work in China.

The Co-Workers
of Mother Teresa

While they are not called to the same lifestyle as the Missionaries of Charity, the lay Co-Workers of Mother Teresa share the same vision of seeing God in every human being. Guided by that vision, they desire to share themselves and their resources with the lonely, the poor, the bereaved, the suffering, and the unloved. Anyone who shares this vision and call, whatever their religious background, may become a Co-Worker.

The Co-Workers of Mother Teresa are not an organization, but a family spanning the globe. There are no dues or collection of funds. The officers are called links. Co-Workers are presently active in seventy countries. If they live near a house of the Missionaries of Charity, the Co-Workers take part in the works of mercy of the Sisters; if not, they join together to carry out works of mercy for those in their own area. Sick and Suffering Co-

Workers who are unable to assist in works of mercy, offer up their own sufferings, uniting them to the work of the Missionaries of Charity. Certain daily prayers are suggested for Co-Workers, including "The Peace Prayer of St. Francis of Assisi."

Anyone interested in knowing more about the Co-Workers may write to:

Ms. Vicki Schmidt
National Link—U.S.A.
Co-Workers of Mother Teresa
8 Stardust Drive
Sherman, Illinois 62684

Photo Credits

Other Books of Interest by Mother Teresa

Loving Jesus

Mother Teresa shares the heart of Jesus in a way that will inspire you to love those who are forgotten and neglected—no matter where they live.

The needy and the poor, she insists, are not only those in our inner-city slums and Third World countries, but those who suffer spiritually or physically in our own families and neighborhoods—an unappreciated spouse, a neglected child, or a lonely shut-in. £3.50

Heart of Joy

These are the writings and teachings of a woman whose works and words have touched more people than any other woman living today. £2.99

One Heart Full of Love

More stirring addresses and interviews given by Mother Teresa to her Missionaries of Charity and other groups worldwide on such topics as self-giving, the call to love our neighbor, and spiritual poverty in the West. £2.99

Available at your Christian bookstore